T0142622

Nobody Likes Monday

Written and illustrated by Alisa Lynn Martin

AuthorHouse™
1663 Liberty Drive
Bloomington, IN 47403
www.authorhouse.com
Phone: 833-262-8899

Because of the dynamic nature of the Internet, any web addresses or links contained in this book may have changed
since publication and may no longer be valid. The views expressed in this work are solely those of the author and do
not necessarily reflect the views of the publisher, and the publisher hereby disclaims any responsibility for them.

Any people depicted in stock imagery provided by Getty Images are models,
and such images are being used for illustrative purposes only.
Certain stock imagery © Getty Images.

This book is printed on acid-free paper.

ISBN: 979-8-8230-0443-5 (sc)
ISBN: 979-8-8230-0444-2 (e)

Library of Congress Control Number: 2023905599

Print information available on the last page.

Published by AuthorHouse 03/31/2023

authorHOUSE®

Nobody Likes Monday

Dedicated to my two beautiful children Meiya and Logan.

Hello, my name is Monday.

Maybe you've heard about me. If you did, I'm sure it wasn't good.

Whenever I come around all I hear is...
Oh No!
Blah, Blah, Blah

Not Again,

and you got to be kidding me!

You see. Nobody
likes Monday!

My Brother Tuesday is an okay guy. He gets the week to a stronger start he says when I pass by.

My sister Wednesday gives everyone hope. Hoping the week goes by in a float.

And Thursday well...

Some say he has tunnel vision and can see the end of the week from far away.

Of course, there is Friday. People can't wait to see him, "you know." Especially when the day has come.

At last, there is Saturday and Sunday. To me they are mom and dad. They always sit together and are always hand in hand.

But Nobody likes
Monday and that
makes me sad.

I wish I too wasn't so so bad.

My mommy reminds me of how much I'm loved.

She says, grown ups were once children who once loved Monday too and loved going to school as much as you.

But as time passed by and they got older. Monday whom they used to love, now just makes them smolder.

Just know it has nothing to do with you and that you are still loved by many too.

We just have to find the beauty in each and everyday and make it special in every way.

The End.

Color in your favorite day of the week

About the Author

Alisa Martin is the Author and Illustrator of the book, "Nobody Likes Monday." Alisa is also a mother of two and is a Childhood Educator. She has worked with children for 11 years and still counting. Alisa found her inspiration to write this story not only by her own children but by also singing and teaching her own class. Every Monday I am welcomed with hugs and smiles from the children. We as adults may dread Mondays but we must remember to make each day count.

Printed in the United States
by Baker & Taylor Publisher Services